Behind a Father's Eyes

Moments in Life through a Father's Eyes

By

Richard Clay Forbes

WESTVIEW BOOK PUBLISHING, INC., NASHVILLE, TENNESSEE

© 2008 by Richard Forbes.

All Rights Reserved. No portion of this book may be reproduced in any fashion, either mechanically or electronically, without the express written permission of the author. Short excerpts may be used with the permission of the author or the publisher for the purposes of media reviews.

First Edition, January 2008

Printed in the United States of America on acid-free paper.

ISBN 1-933912-86-3

Cover design by Richard Forbes and Landon Earps

Typography by Mary Catharine Nelson

Prepress by Westview Book Publishing, Inc.

WESTVIEW BOOK PUBLISHING, INC.
P.O. Box 210183
Nashville, Tennessee 37221
www.westviewpublishing.com

Dedicated To

This book is dedicated to my lovely wife Ann, and my wonderful children. The riches they have given me are immeasurable and the memories priceless.

I would also like to thank my dear friend, Colonel Wayland Parker, for encouraging me to publish what I previously had shared with family and friends alone.

Richard Clay Forbes

Contents

INTRODUCTION vii

BEHIND A FATHER'S EYES viii

THE MILITARY AND THEIR FAMILIES 1

FROM SO FAR AWAY 2
OUR FLAG 4
QUIET NIGHT IN ARLINGTON 6
A SOLITARY DRUMMER 8
WARRIOR KNIGHTS 10
HUSH A BYE 12
A SOLDIER'S LULLABY 14
THE PRICE THAT WAS PAID 16
THE ARCH 18
HEIRS OF LIBERTY 20

OUR HEAVENLY FATHER 23

GIFT OF LOVE 24
THE PRODIGAL SON 26
SUNDAY NIGHT REVIVAL 28
THE WISDOM OF OUR FATHER 30
THE ONES YOU TOOK AWAY 32
SOMETIMES WE NEED GOD TO HAVE SKIN ON HIM 34
DARK OF NIGHT 36
GOD LOVES US ALL THE SAME 38
CHRISTMAS 40

ON DEATH AND MOURNING 43

I HAVEN'T TOLD YOU OFTEN ENOUGH 44
WHEN I LEAVE THIS BODY 46
THE MEADOW 48
HE'S GONE 50

THE LOVE HIS CHILDREN SHARE	52
THIS LAST MILE	54
GREEN GRASS	56
PURE AND WHITE	58

SPORTS 61

SPIRIT WINGS	62
A YOUNG MAN STANDS IN FOOTBALL SPIKES	64
THUNDER IN THE GROUND	66
WITH YOU	68
CHILKOOT PASS	70
COACH PALMER	72
HEAVENLY RUGBY	74

FAMILY, LOVE, AND SUCH 77

PIRATES OF WHITE COUNTY	78
LITTLE BOYS INSIDE	80
ALL NIGHT COALS	82
I SLEEP ALONE WITH YOU AT NIGHT	84
HE THOUGHT SHE LOVED HIM	86
SMALL THINGS	88
HER QUIET HOUSE	90
THE WHIPPOORWILL	92
TWENTY-FOUR YEARS IN THE MAKING	94
A GLIMPSE OF HEAVEN	96
GRANDMA'S SONG	98
Y'ALL BE SMART NOW	100
UNCLE WADE	102
WITH HIS BOOTS ON	104
LET HIM SEE THROUGH YOUR EYES	106

TO MY FATHER 109

THE NIGHT MY HERO DIED	110

Introduction

It seems that as you get older, it is easier to let some of the more personal feelings bubble to the surface. Men in general, and Fathers in particular, hold a great deal inside and I hope that through this work you will better understand what travels through their consciousness.

Everyone has a certain rhythm that flows within them. Musicians have melody, singers have verse, and woodcarvers have images that come alive in wood. Poetry is the rhythm of my life; it is as natural as breath.

These poems were inspired by friends, family, and the happenings of the time. I have included a short description of the event or thought that led to the writing of each poem. I hope that, in some small way, they shed light on your life and possibly make you smile, cry, or help you see your father differently.

These are the thoughts that perk through the mind of that complex human figure called Father.

Behind a Father's Eyes

Who's this man looking back at me
From under bushy brows of gray
A distant sparkle glimmering;
Morning star against the day

Behind a father's eyes you glimpse
Bits of the gentle soul inside
That he reveals so stubbornly
These feelings he's long denied

I see him truly when he smiles
While holding his granddaughter sweet
Or lifting tiny grandson high
In his hand he holds both feet

Age allows him the luxury
To reveal what he once hid
A softness that he put away
When whiskers transformed the kid

The Military and Their Families

From So Far Away

When the war in Iraq started, we almost immediately started hearing about those who had been killed. This was terrible news, but I also knew that it was only a piece of the story. Everyone associated with the military understands that for each soldier killed there are many who are wounded.

My father was a retired army officer (two purple hearts) and my mother still goes to Walter Reed Army Hospital in Washington D.C. when she needs medical attention. One afternoon while talking with her, she described to me the young soldiers in wheel chairs that had been brought outside the hospital to enjoy the sun. All of them had been wounded in Iraq or Afghanistan.

The more I thought of those young soldiers and the sacrifices they made for our country, the more I felt a need to put into words their ordeal. What better way to tell their story than through a love poem.

From So Far Away

Can you hear me call your name from so far away
As I watch the night ignite and the tracers sway
Do you feel me tremble as the canon roar in might
With each streaming rocket can you see my face tonight

I hold your memory close to me, loving you so slow
Then I jump from safety into battle's vicious flow
Do you feel me tremble as the canon roar in might
With each streaming rocket can you see my face tonight

Are your dreams filled with the vision of our parting night
While I squat behind this hulk engaged in deadly fight
Do you feel me tremble as the canon roar in might
With each streaming rocket can you see my face tonight

I feel your touch, I hear your voice, gentle in my mind
The morphine rushes to my head; leaving wounds behind
Do you feel me tremble as the canon roar in might
With each streaming rocket can you see my face tonight

Window's light shines on me standing silent in the street
Seeking strength to take a step, homecoming bitter sweet
Do you feel me tremble as the canon roar in might
With each streaming rocket can you see my face tonight

Will you love this soldier when I knock upon your door
Hoping you will recognize the one that you adore
Do you feel me tremble as the canon roar in might
With each streaming rocket can you see my face tonight

Our Flag

My son-in-law came home from Iraq for two weeks of rest and relaxation (R&R). It was a great two weeks as I watched him hold his year old daughter that he hadn't seen since she was two months old, and hug and kiss my daughter as if no one else were there.

His uniform was spotless and the patch of the 101st Airborne Division and our flag were prominent on his sleeve. It was then that the inspiration for *Our Flag* came upon me. He probably wondered why I asked him so often about our flag and where it was displayed at his Forward Operating Base. I already knew from pictures that he had sent home that it hung above his cot, right next to pictures of Holly and baby Jane Ann.

After Josh had returned to Iraq, I was sitting on the back deck with Jane Ann when the words came to me in a rush.

Our Flag

He hugged his family at the airport
As his flight prepared to leave
Held them in strong arms
Flag sewn on uniform sleeve

Now he's in Tikrit Iraq
With our flag upon his truck
Hoping on this mission
His vehicle won't be struck

When his day is over
And he walks to evening meal
The path leads him between two flags
Love of home is all he feels

Sweating underneath our flag
He lays his head at night
It hangs upon his barracks wall
To remind him why he fights

As he slumbers restlessly
A comrade returns home
Lying still beneath our flag
To rest, but not alone

I sit safe on my back porch
Flag fluttering in the breeze
Granddaughter in my lap
Lord protect her father please

Each time I see old glory
Waving proud upon its pole
Tears come to my eyes
For the soldiers who pay our toll

Quiet Night in Arlington

I saw an award winning photograph of Marines removing a flag draped coffin from an airplane and it brought back vivid images of my father's burial at Arlington National Cemetery. I was lost for a time in that memory and the impact that Arlington had on me.

The Marines were working at night and the lighted faces of the passengers could be seen clearly in the windows of the plane. Somehow this took me to *A Quiet Night in Arlington* and the words met me there.

There is something about a National Cemetery that transcends our ability to grasp. There is an aura that can only be felt, or talked around. There is no real way of describing this wholly in words.

Quiet Night in Arlington

In the twilight's fading light
Do they form in ranks once more
Practicing for the faithful march
When called to distant shore

Can we hear them bark "Dress Right!"
When the night wind settles still
See their breath as drifting fog
In the low beneath the hill

Is there reverence in the voices
As "Eyes Right" echoes from stones
Every eye turning towards the hill
To welcome back unknowns

Are presidents watching proudly
These men that they once mourned
Saluting as they pass them by
Honor hardships they have born

Will the labor of marines be heard
As they plant our flag on high
Above a sleeping city
Monument's light against the sky

Does the quiet night in Arlington
Come alive with heroes past
Reliving lives to duty bound
Standing watch until the last

The guard changes reverently each night
At the tomb of the unknown
The click of heels across the graves
Marching solemn with their own

A Solitary Drummer

I attended the Virginia Military Institute long, long ago. It was (and still is) a place lost in time. It is a Spartan life where honor, loyalty, and love of country rule supreme. For the grueling process of forming cadets, the Institute uses an instrument called the ratline.

The ratline is a system in which incoming students (Rats) are challenged mentally, physically, and emotionally. They are subservient to every cadet. This system would seem barbaric to those un-indoctrinated souls who haven't experienced it. Yet, the end product is a group of men who are bound to each other in a way that is hard to describe. The byproduct is a love for the very Institute that took them through this test by fire.

Years have passed since I left VMI, but the bond is still strong and the loyalty I have for my Brother Rats is without question. Although I don't typically, or at least consciously, think about it, I live by the principles of the Institute and maintain the attachment to my classmates.

One afternoon I received an email from my class president (yes, he is still my class president). One of my fellow classmates had lost his son to cancer. I was immediately struck with a sense of empathy and loss. This young man, like his father had been, was a cadet at VMI. He followed the tradition like so many before him.

I thought about his father and my mind wandered to all the VMI men who had preceded him into death. You see, there is a certain call that VMI men (and now women) hear. They march to a different drummer, even into death.

A Solitary Drummer

Far across House Mountain
In a distant glen
A solitary drummer
Calls for VMI men.

From night's silent slumber
Or battle's raging din
A solitary drummer
Calls for VMI men.

Gathering in the clearing
Waiting for "Fall In"
A solitary drummer
Calls for VMI men.

Fathers, sons, and brothers
Suffering at an end
A solitary drummer
Calls for VMI men.

All will hear the drum roll
Somewhere deep within
A solitary drummer
Calls for VMI men.

Warrior Knights

Following the events of 9/11 when the United States went to war in Afghanistan, it was personal for me in a different way than for many people. I didn't lose a loved one in the World Trade Center Towers, although it felt like I had, nor did I know someone who was killed at the Pentagon or on Flight 93.

What made this personal for me was my college roommate from the Virginia Military Institute. Colonel Wayland Parker, my friend and roommate left his wife and daughter to stand in harms way for me and my family. This is a debt I can never repay, and not surprisingly, a debt he doesn't believe I owe him.

A day didn't go by that I didn't think of my friend and our other native sons and daughters who fought the Taliban. I wrote *Warrior Nights* for our friends, family, and roommates who answered their nation's call.

Warrior Knights

When nations quake on peril's edge
Citizens huddling on precipitous ledge
A cry goes out for a savior's intercession
Valiant rescue and steadfast protection

The call is answered by a noble breed
Who stand at ready and respond to need
From shadowed obscurity they do spring
Warrior Knights, dealing sword's slashing sting

Their blood and lives without reservation
Placed at the feet of a grateful nation
Into battle with great courage and might
Crimson are their days, and amber the night

A nation stands breathless, a price is paid
By the warriors of freedom fair Sir and Maid
Bold is their spirit yet gentle the heart
Justice not vengeance sets them apart

Danger abated and peace once more won
They return to their perch the job well done
A people solemnly lay the dead to rest
America's finest, our nation's best

But when the storms rage and fear rules the night
The call will go out for the soldier's might
Swift from the shadows the heroes will rise
With resolute cause, and fire in their eyes.

Hush a Bye

I watch the news religiously each morning. It is an integral part of my morning ritual and besides giving me something to do while I drink that first cup of coffee, it brings me up to date on world happenings. Often there will be stories that will move me and those regarding our troops in Iraq always bring me out of my caffeine starved stupor.

Hearing morning after morning the report of "one marine was killed yesterday" or "two army soldiers were killed last night", weighed heavily on my heart. I would think of my 19 year old son and wonder how those families were dealing with the news of their son or daughter's loss.

As a father it seemed natural to worry about how the other members of my family would react to such a sorrowful event. I wondered how my wife would cope with news such as this. Not unlike most mothers, her life is wrapped around our children.

One morning while my heart was going out to the families of these brave men and women, *Hush a Bye* started flowing into me.

Hush a Bye

Slipping from her bed at the sound of a little cry;
Changes his wet diaper, gotta keep him dry.
Mama rocks her baby in the middle of the night
Sings him "Hush a Bye, everything's gonna be alright."

Running down the school hall; can't wait to give it a try;
She goes back to the car to have a first day cry.
Mama misses her boy in the middle of the night
Sings him "Hush a Bye, everything's gonna be alright"

Playing football on Friday night, son takes quite a lick.
She covers her eyes, she can't look, almost makes her sick
Mama sooths her athlete in the middle of the night;
Tells him "Close your eyes, everything's gonna be alright"

He leaves tomorrow for boot camp to make himself a man;
All her pleading was for naught, on his own he'll stand.
Mama loses her young man in the middle of the night
Begs him "stay safe son, everything's gonna be alright"

The officer says "your son has died" in far away Iraq;
Father holds his weeping wife as dark night turns to black.
Mama mourns her soldier in the middle of the night
Prays "Lord hold my baby, and everything's gonna be alright"

She places his purple heart in her precious box
Alongside his first tooth and a clipping of his locks
Mama lays him to rest in the middle of the night
says "I'll see you soon, everything's gonna be alright"

She fetches a tattered blanket from its keeping place;
Sits slowly in her rocker, holds it gently to her face.
Mama rocks her baby in the middle of the night
Sings him "Hush a Bye, everything's gonna be alright"

Sings him "Hush a Bye, everything's gonna be alright"

A Soldier's Lullaby

Joshua, my son-in-law is a member of the Kentucky National Guard. He was called to active duty and informed that his unit was being deployed to Iraq. Joshua and my daughter Holly had been married less that a year and their daughter was only two months old. Needless to say, this young family was going to experience a trial like none other.

Joshua trained in Greenville, Kentucky and at Fort Dix in New Jersey. By the time Thanksgiving came Joshua had been away for three months. His unit was given leave and allowed to go home before they took the long flight to Iraq. I drove my daughter and granddaughter to the airport to meet him. The scene was touching and wonderful.

For four days Joshua, Holly, and baby Jane Ann were together again. Both sets of parents were there to spend these brief days with Joshua and family. It was a time of celebration and thanking God that he had allowed him to come home prior to going to war. Yet, in the back of every mind was the reality that we wouldn't see him again for at least a year.

The time passed quickly and soon I was in the car taking them back to the airport. Joshua sat between his girls and looked back and forth at them as if he were trying to etch their faces into his memory. I tried to sit quietly and not intrude on these last few minutes.

We reached the airport and goodbyes were said. Hugs, kisses, and tears. Joshua kept turning to look back at Holly and Jane Ann as he walked toward the terminal. It ripped me to pieces as I stood silently watching.

It was a somber trip home. My mind wandered to Joshua, Holly, and Iraq. What would he be thinking when he thought of Holly? How would he handle the separation and the longing for home? *A Soldier's Lullaby* was born.

A Soldier's Lullaby

I lay her picture on my pillow
Close my eyes, pretend she's there.
Breathe in deep to smell the fragrance
Of the jasmine in her hair.

Somewhere across that ocean
My sweet lover sleeps tonight.
Does she know I'm thinking of her
In the fading desert light?

Is my picture on her pillow?
Is she lying next to me?
When she closes her eyes to dream,
Is that soft sigh just for me?

Tomorrow morning I'll awaken,
Wipe the sand out of my eyes.
But tonight across that ocean
A soldier sings a lullaby.

Sleep now my loving baby
Close your eyes and don't you cry
My head is on your pillow
Our lover's moon is in the sky

We'll be together until morning
When the birds sing sweet to you
About a soldier's quiet tear drops
Lying on your grass like dew

The Price That Was Paid

During my lifetime the political posture of the country has changed dramatically. The days of a politician taking an unfavorable stance based on personal belief is over. Many citizens are looking strictly at what's in it for them. Judges are making law from the bench. It just seems to me that as a country we have lost sight of the vision our founding fathers had.

I don't recall the incident, but it could have been one of any number of morning news stories that gave life to *The Price That Was Paid*. Sometimes we need to express our frustration and question the direction things are moving in. Maybe that one voice will resonate.

The Price That Was Paid

Do we understand the price that was paid
So that we can enjoy freedom today?
Do we understand the sacrifices made
When the foundation of freedom was laid?

The news says trillions, we don't blink an eye,
But when it's our money, then hear us cry.
When a soldier is laid still in his grave
Is it different when it's kin we gave?

We watch Senators vote their party's line
Regardless the bill, the same every time.
Do they understand the sacrifices made,
Or just the party boss as freedoms fade.

I see the judges make their rulings
No pledge, no God, in our children's schooling.
Do they understand the price that was paid
By those who fought that this would be saved?

When a soldier is laid still in his grave
Is it different when it's kin we gave?
Do we understand the debt we just paid
Before it's our loved one taken in trade?

When asked to defend the freedoms hard won
Think long before turning away
It may be your voice, a single one,
That honors the life of a patriot son.

The Arch

On the night of August 24th, 1970, I was sitting with my parents watching the evening news. The war in Vietnam filled the airways and conversation. The mood was mixed, with my parents facing the somber realization that this would be my last night at home for quite some time, and me feeling the excited yet fearful anticipation of a challenging new adventure.

The morning of August 25th came earlier than I wanted, but we ate a quiet breakfast and I kissed my mother goodbye, not realizing that I would never see her again through those same youthful eyes.

My father and I made the four hour drive into the mountains of Virginia with little conversation. He was a quiet person by nature and in retrospect, I realize that he already knew what I was about to undertake.

When we pulled the truck into the Virginia Military Institute I saw the castle-looking campus for the first time. It was beautiful, but at the same time, had a cold and intimidating air to it.

We walked into Cocke Hall, an old but immaculately maintained gymnasium, and as my father completed the forms that parents must, I signed my name into "The Book", and was escorted out of the gym with a group of boys who looked equally awed, and frightened.

We were led single file up a flight of concrete stairs, overlooked by ancient French cannons, to an Archway into barracks. I could hear shouting inside and immediately felt the sweat on my forehead. My life was about to change forever.

May 2nd, 2006 - I was struck dumb by the news that Ken Dennett, a VMI classmate, had passed away. I thought back on all the times I had sat in class with him, or passed him smiling on the barracks stoop. This triggered memories of my VMI experience. It was a pivotal moment in the lives of the young boys who became men there.

I thought of my Brother Rats, and the words and imagery coursed through me. I wrote *The Arch* for my BRs, but it could very well tell the story of many others as they made passage into manhood after marching through those hallowed arches.

The Arch

Through the arch one August day
We walked where few boys dared
Frightened sweat stood on our face
Left behind all those who cared

Reciting chants and mystic facts
Sleeping nights upon the hay
Till drums rolled deep like thunder
Ghost voices warned not to say

Somewhere in the chaos came
Trembling whispers of like kind
Little rats were gathering close
For survival we would bind

Slowly in that ancient forge
Our metal was beaten pure
Tempered to withstand a blow
Too sharp to be endured

Men marched through the arches where
Hopeful boys once walked in fright
Glanced back at a war torn world
Yelled "All Right Sir!" to the night

Years passed by and boys would come
Shaking to that age old beat
Hear our scream in nightmare's grip
Till made pure by forge's heat

Then with heads held high to see
Dressed sharp in all our starches
We formed together one last time;
The men who march through arches

Now though time has taken much
In dreams I hear "Forward Harch!"
And see lost faces, Brother Rats;
Brave young boys who dared the arch

Heirs of Liberty

I spent an evening with a retired Marine Corps Gunnery Sergeant. Among his numerous decorations are two Bronze Stars, and a Silver Star for valor, as well as three Purple Hearts. To say that he has given himself in the service of our country would be an understatement. During our conversation he casually mentioned that he needed an operation to remove a piece of shrapnel from behind his left eye to save his eyesight. This is just another day for "Gunny."

We talked into the wee hours of the morning and our conversation led us in many directions. When I finally lay down in bed, I shed quiet tears for him, and men like him. It may sound insignificant to some, but when he referred to the Marines in Iraq who had been lost under his command (37 in all) as "My Marines," it struck me hard. This is a man who takes young soldiers under his wing; the kind of man that America's sons look up to. This is a man who views those under his command as his personal responsibility; His Marines.

The next morning I was thinking back on our evening, and it suddenly struck me that I had always known him, or at least men like him. Gunny had the same motivation and heroic patriotism that I saw in my own father. Although these two men were separated by generations and services, their basic belief in liberty, country, men, and mission were the same. It occurred to me that I was an heir of the liberty they had bled and risked their lives for. I wrote *Heirs of Liberty* from my point of view, as a child born to an Army Infantryman, but precious liberty is purchased daily for ALL of us by many men and women such as these.

Heirs of Liberty

I am the military child;
Born of a mother; lying alone in hospital ward
Father under battle's haze;
muddy roads lined with hard men.

I am the son of a warrior;
Eyes having seen too much; of what shames peace.
Startling awake at night;
Eyes franticly search death's blow.

I am the pall mourner;
Once naïve; slain innocence stains fields bold red.
Struggling to win next breath
Against those fighting for same.

I am the heir of liberty;
Longed for, Bled for; stoked by Mother's lost hopes.
Liberty's price; our youth;
Arm hangs for hallowed ground.

I am the guardian of honor;
Heaped upon graves, valiant men; too oft forgotten.
Innocent children play unaware,
Our flag; the patriot's sacred banner

Our Heavenly Father

Gift of Love

Contemplating the emotion of love, and what a wonderful gift it is, spawned a series of revelations. This overpowering emotion is the result of our being created in the image of God. It is a bit of God passed to us at creation and is a wonderful part of what we can expect in heaven.

God loves us, even before we're born. Isn't that a magnificent realization?

Gift of Love

How can we love a baby
Nestled deep within the womb,
Or a man we've never seen
Dining in the upper room

God made us in his image
Blessed us with his holy grace
Gave us love beyond all reason;
An Unworthy human race

He's our father, He's our Lord
He's the love within our hearts
Taking root in infant soil
Before groaning labor starts

So praise him, hallelujah!
For the love we feel today
Praise him, hallelujah!
With emotion when we pray.

Love survives the lonely grave
Never fading from within
Some say that it is over
But in him it just begins

His spirit is our ointment
His love for evermore
Jesus, Lord and Savior
Guiding light on distant shore

He's our brother. He's our king
He's the hope of life in rain
Showering love upon us
Soothing all our grief and pain

So let's praise him, hallelujah!
For the love we feel today
Praise him, hallelujah!
With emotion when we pray.

The Prodigal Son

Sometimes the most routine occurrences in our daily lives can send our thoughts wandering. I was taking just such a journey when I wrote *The Prodigal Son.*

Driving down West End Avenue in Nashville, it isn't uncommon to see a homeless soul who is obviously drunk. I have often found myself wondering what their story is; what set of life events brought them to this sorrowful state? Was it alcohol, a lost love, mental illness, or some obscure set of circumstances?

Being an optimist, I always hope that there will be an end to their cold, hungry, drunken existence. As a Christian I know that God can lift even the most wretched and return them to him. I also realize that there is an earthly price attached to sin.

You have probably seen homeless people in your town or city. Have you ever pondered the road that might have brought them to this place, or where life will lead them from here?

The Prodigal Son

I lost sight of paradise
In a bottle of scotch and a little ice
Never knew how fast a man could sink,
What he would do for another drink

Hit rock bottom in San Antone
No one there to take me home
Holes in my clothes and a mouth full of paste
Nearly killed a man for another taste

Who'd have thought that you'd be there
When I'd lost everything I had to wear
Left you standing by your car
Loved you still, but had gone too far

I wasn't looking, so he must have been,
When Jesus found me in all my sin
Empty bottle in my hand
Cracks in my lips and shoes full of sand

What would make him reach that low
To save a bum no one cared to know
But he touched my soul and changed my life
Eased my burden and healed the strife

He took the bottle from my hand
Lifted me up, made a drunk a man
I could tell you about the prodigal son
But when you look at me, you see one

The hurt I caused you I can't erase
But that is a sorrow I must face
Jesus has saved me on the cross
But my sin on earth has come at a cost

Now I'm standing here at your door
Not asking you to love me any more
But begging your forgiveness for all I've done
That has hurt you so deeply, and our young son.

Sunday Night Revival

Having married into a Pentecostal family, it didn't take me long to experience a good old fashion Holy Ghost Revival. It is an experience that can change your life and entertain you at the same time. My favorite part of the entire affair is its simplicity. The message is straight forward, the music is easy to sing along with, and the atmosphere is charged.

Thinking back on the early years of my marriage and how different life was then, led me to a warm summer night on the church pew and revival. I remember Ann with our young children and that wonderful feeling of anticipation. There were no pretenses here, everyone was a brother or sister in Christ (and if they weren't now, they would be by the end of the evening).

Somehow these memories always bask in a golden light. They are warm and wonderful. It was in this semi dream that I wrote the tongue in cheek recollection called *Sunday Night Revival*.

Sunday Night Revival

Never before has there been such a sight
As a band of angels suddenly taking flight
Above the choir on a summer Sunday night
While the church is rocking and the preacher gets right

Pastor in the pulpit sweating out a sermon
Looking straight at me but calling me Herman
Everyone thinks he is speaking to them
But that preacher knows he's shouting bout him

Deacons are answering with a loud AMEN
As the message strikes deep to the heart of sin
Little Mrs. Johnson jumps from her seat
Shouts "Save Me Jesus" and swoons in the heat

Sister Sue dances up and down the aisle
Eyes closed tight arms waving with a smile
Mamas are nursing babies on the pew
Children at their feet with nary a shoe

"Every eye closed, can you hear Jesus calling?"
The alter fills with everyone bawling
From high above the Holy Ghost falls
And the sound of tongues echoes in the halls

Sing me a verse of that age old song
One more round it won't take long
Mama grab the babies and head to the door
We'll be back tomorrow evening for more

Never before has there been such a sight
As a band of angels suddenly taking flight
Above the choir on a summer Sunday night
While the church is rocking and the preacher gets right

The Wisdom of Our Father

The loss of a parent changes you. I received the news of my father's death and began to mourn, but seeing him lying in his coffin drove the reality home. I was suddenly filled with a deep sense of loss and the need to understand why he was gone.

My father had suffered through heart surgery, strokes, and then crippling bone degeneration. He was 83 years old and had obviously been failing, but he was my Dad. I felt abandoned, alone. We buried him and I was sure that this would bring closure, but it didn't come. I slipped into depression.

During a quiet time in my office, searching for the reason he had been taken from me, I began to pray. I took my grief back to my core, my rock, my savior. Suddenly the words began to come again and I wrote *The Wisdom of Our father*. I didn't receive the reason why that I was searching for, what I received was much more, comfort and hope.

The Wisdom of Our Father

I looked down at my Daddy, a shadow of the man
Who swatted my rear, wiped my nose, and held my little hand.
I cried the tears of yesteryear till my eyes turned bright red
and asked him why he left me alone as I stroked his ashen head.

I remembered Jesus on the cross and it all came back, you see,
He looked up to the heavens and cried "why have you forsaken me."
I thought about his father who watched as he hung there
And realized that he loved him and just how much he cared.

Daddy is with Jesus; he died as we all must.
He's with my savior at the throne; in God I place my trust.
One day soon I'll kneel beside the man who earned my love
And thank the Lord for the words he spoke to his father above.

When the day comes to see Jesus and visit with my Dad
I hope my precious children find comfort in what Christ said
And know that the love of our father, though sometimes a mystery,
Is surrounded by a wisdom that is often hard to see.

Jesus died on the cross, he died as we all must,
As man he had been born, molded from the dust.
To save men like my father, like me, and like my son,
He gave his life for each of us then uttered "it is done."

The Ones You Took Away

Sometimes in our walk with the Lord, we find ourselves asking God for certain gifts that we perceive will make us happy. As a father of four, I have often had to weigh the requests of my children. Quite often, what they want and what they need are two very different things. It is much the same in our religious development.

One morning I was thinking about how this played itself out in my life and wrote *The Ones You Took Away*. I borrowed experiences of my own and folded them into those of my parent's generation to tell this story from a slightly different perspective.

Eventually (one hopes), we realize that there can be love in saying no, and meaning in simple gifts.

The Ones You Took Away

An old man with a walker
Shuffled down the aisle to pray,
I knelt down close beside him
Just to hear what he would say.

He said "God I want to thank you for
Your gifts to me each day,
But most of all, thank you Lord,
For the ones you took away.

You gave me two fine legs,
A back so straight and strong,
Eyes sharp as an eagle's,
Calloused hands and muscled arms

But thank you Lord for swapping them
For those I have tonight
They're suited for your purpose
And perfect in your sight."

I turned my head to see him
And his eyes were squinted tight
He'd dropped down to his knees,
His bowed body looked so slight.

I wondered "who's this man
So humble and so frail
Who can pray with such power
That it sets my soul to sail?"

He wept softly beside me
His body shook and sobbed
Then he raised his arms before him
His strength was nearly robbed.

"My legs led me down twisted roads,
My back was straight in pride,
My eyes were fixed on gold,
Hands and arms on the wrong side.

Now my legs have found their knees
And my back is bent in prayer,
My eyes can see your glory,
And my arms can feel you there."

He said "God I want to thank you for
Your gifts to me each day,
But most of all, thank you Lord,
For the ones you took away."

I never saw that man again
But I know who brought him there
To teach me about heavenly gifts
Through an old man's simple prayer.

I pray, "God I want to thank you for
Your gifts to me each day,
But most of all, thank you Lord
For the ones you took away."

Sometimes We Need God to Have Skin on Him

I was exchanging emails with my pastor Dan Scott and was telling him about some trials I had been through in my religious life. He has a wonderful knack for saying exactly what you need to hear at just the right moment, and true to form he gave me his uplifting testimony, and advice.

What Dan didn't realize was that his parting observation would turn into a poem. I loved his comment and used it as my title when I wrote *Sometimes We Need God to Have Skin on Him*.

Sometimes We Need God to Have Skin on Him

Sometimes we need God to have skin on him
To touch our souls with human hands
Maybe from close by, or from distant lands
But, sometimes we need God to have human hands

Like a surgeon he bares our innermost sin
He can lead us to his side, reborn again
Saved by grace and an unwitting friend
Sometimes we need God to have skin on him

When our hearts are broken and spirit thin
Sailing rough seas with the light growing dim
He'll send us a captain to put our sails in trim
Sometimes we need God to have skin on him

Thank God for the servants he uses to touch
The spirits of those who need it so much
When the limbs of faith are broken, twisted, and such
Thank God for his grace that gives us a crutch

Dark of Night

After reading a somewhat disturbing sermon on the effects of spiritual depression (Ecclesiastes 2), I wanted to express what I felt was the crux of the dissertation. A separation from God is a miserable feeling, but once that relationship has been reestablished, the cure is almost immediate. There is a sudden influx of joy that one doesn't want to ever lose.

Dark of Night

I stumbled in the dark of night
Lay mournful on cold ground
Wanting not to see again
Or hear life's droning sound

He comes for me, lamp in hand
Lifts me to my feet
Gives me verse to fill my ears
Music warm and sweet

Oh my soul rejoicing
Joy flows forth within
My breast is full to bursting
Vanquished now the sin

My spirit calls for angels
Carry me to his side
Singing words I know not
On a melody they ride

Never more the dark of night
Never more the cold
Never more be blinded
His glory to be told

God Loves Us All The Same

I am always inspired by the writing of Dan Scott, and his sermon titled "When the Dream Finds a Dreamer" was no exception. Dan was using 1st Samuel 3:1-10 to press home our need to be receptive to God's Dream for us. He further elaborated on the fact that people in the church have different gifts that can all be used to glorify God and fulfill his dream for us and our church.

After reading Dan's sermon, I was mulling over his message when the need to write overcame me. I wrote *God Loves Us All The Same* as an expression of my emotion at that moment. Perhaps you will also sense a bit of the animal lover in me as well.

God Loves Us All The Same

I had two puppies when I was young
Different as night and day
One did tricks by the bushel
The other couldn't learn to stay.

They both met me at the door
Every day when I came home
The smart one sat waiting for a pat
The other mauled me like a bone

I loved them both just the same
And hugged them to my face
One liked to do his tricks for me
The other liked to run and chase

When I wanted to romp and play
There was a playmate just for me
And when I wanted to impress a friend
There were tricks for all to see.

The boy in me is now long gone
And my puppies have passed away
But I learned a lesson from them
That I value still today

Each of us has a special gift
And God loves us all the same
So that when he has a job to do
He can call us out by name.

Christmas

As a Christian, Christmas is a special time. It isn't simply a holiday shopping experience, as the retail industry would have us believe. It isn't a Christmas tree decorated with twinkling lights. It isn't lavish gifts or diner parties. Somewhere along the line our society began stripping the simple yet wonderful message that our savior was born from Christmas.

As I watched a sign being erected at a local park which read "Holiday Tree Recycling" I was struck with the sad realization that our society was collectively losing its soul. I sat down and wrote *Christmas* for my family. I wanted us to reaffirm our belief that this was a celebration of the birth of Jesus Christ. The story is simple just as Jesus' carpenter status in human life was simple. He was born in a barn, wrapped in swaddling cloth, and laid in a manger. He suffered and without us asking, gave himself to be crucified and die for our sins.

Christmas

For the seekers there shown a star
Bright in the winter sky
Leading them to a precious place
A newborn baby's cry

With gifts they trekked the desert night
To kneel before a king
And welcome the Lord of Lords
While angels hovered to sing

Adorned in swaddling cloth and straw
In a manger he was laid
No crown to grace his precious head
A pauper he was made

His kingdom was not of the earth
In heaven he would reign
And sit at his father's hand
The lamb from death and pain

So we celebrate this day
A gift of life received
Holy Father gave his son
That sin could be relieved

Behind a Father's Eyes

On Death and Mourning

I Haven't Told You Often Enough

There are moments in our lives where a tragic event in another's life seems to bleed over into our own. The death of a young man named Christopher was just such an event. Christopher died of brain cancer at the age of 24. His father is my son Jim's Boy Scout Troop Leader, Paul.

Paul is one of those very special people that you count yourself fortunate to have known. He is the father of two sons, yet spends countless hours with the boys of others. He is an Eagle Scout and has dedicated over 20 years to teaching boys what it means to be a Boy Scout and a man. There is no measuring the depth of his love for his sons, yet his gift is so ample that it spills over to every young man who comes into contact with him.

When the news came that Christopher was in his final days, a deep sadness poured over me. I sat in my comfortable chair and wondered to myself; if that were my son, what would I say to him knowing that these might be my last words to him.

I wrote *I Haven't Told You Often Enough* in less than an hour. It came like a well spring from the love for my own sons and for Paul and Chris.

I Haven't Told You Often Enough

I kiss your face and hold your hand as you slip away
But son I have a few last things that I would like to say.

I haven't told you often enough I'm proud you are my son
I cherish all our times together, the memories every one

I haven't told you often enough the joy you bring to me
The love I felt within my heart as you sat upon my knee.

I haven't told you often enough I looked forward to our talks
The questions you would ask me, holding hands while taking walks

I haven't told you often enough that when I corrected you
How it hurt me deep inside but it's something fathers must do

I haven't told you often enough that when you left for school
And came home such a bright young mind it made me feel a fool

I haven't told you often enough that since you've become a man
I'm honored you want to be like me, and humbled that you can

I haven't told you often enough that I love you with all I am
And will until we reunite in the presence of the lamb

Now you'll walk a trail your father has never known
So mark it well that I might follow the path that you have shown.
We will meet in sweet reunion on that distant shore
And walk the trails of heaven from then till ever more.

When I Leave This Body

When friends with young children face a life threatening situation it is especially hard to deal with. When Mike and Elizabeth announced that Elizabeth had been diagnosed with breast cancer, Ann and I were distraught. Ann consoled Elizabeth as best she could, and Mike and I pretended to be strong and reassuring as we talked about the advances in cancer treatment with each other.

The reality is that fathers in specific and men in general don't like to deal openly with the dread, fear, and other feelings associated with news such as this. Retreating to my realistic comfort zone, I worked my way from the worst case scenario to the simple removal of the tumor. What scared me the most however was the idea of leaving one's children.

I worried about Elizabeth and prayed for her healing, but my mind inevitably went back to "What would I do if I knew I was dying". I know that this sounds morbid, but men tend to deal better with concrete happenings, "This is what I'll do" we are far less comfortable with "How do I feel about this". I was more comfortable letting Ann handle the emotion of the situation.

The fact that we don't feel comfortable expressing certain feelings doesn't mean that we don't feel them. I would worry about her quietly. Finally, while sitting in my chair staring blankly at the television, the need to write struck me. For all the children I wrote *When I Leave This Body*.

When I Leave This Body

When I leave this body to heaven go by grace
I pray you'll close your eyes and fondly see my face.

Remember that in time of trouble I'll be standing near
So that when you sigh my name your troubles I will hear.

When life is smiling on you and happiness fills your heart
I will be there watching dear, my smile will not depart.

At your bedside I will stand as night comes closing in,
And you will feel my gentle touch as a summer wind.

When you leave your body to heaven go by grace
I will lead you by the hand to our father's place.

Then we'll stand and watch and guard the loves that you beget
And pray they know that we are near, and never will forget.

The Meadow

After losing my father, I thought a great deal about heaven. As I mulled the concept over in my mind, I was struck by the simplicity of the question "How do we know there's a heaven?" As a Christian adult it seems pretty cut and dried, but how would you explain this to a young person in imagery they could relate to.

I wrote the first two lines of *The Meadow* and sat there for a moment. Nothing was happening; I just didn't feel it. The poem sat in this state for a couple of days until I called my mother to check on her.

During our conversation she began to tell me about some heart problems my cousin was having. This cousin tills my Grandfather's farm in North Carolina just like four generations have done. After I hung up the phone it was as if a gate had opened. Somewhere in my subconscious the block had been removed and a poem was released.

I was back on my Grandfather's farm and was walking with him again. Life always seemed so simple then.

The Meadow

I asked My Daddy one Sunday, when I was still quite young
How do we know that heaven's there when the day is done
And this is what he said to me as he looked out across our farm,
Ran calloused fingers through my hair and took me by the arm

Son There's a meadow on the far side of the hill
From here you just can't see it, but when the wind is still,
You can smell the flowers sweet, and hear the lark call shrill
Although you're not there yet you know it's waiting still

I know your mother's waiting there to greet us when we come
From here you just can't see her, but with each rising sun
I can smell her sweet perfume and hear laughter as she runs
And though we're not there yet she says "I love you son"

So you ask me about heaven and how we know it's there
Well son it's like our meadow and the memories that we share
There's a table set in heaven, prepared for us with care
And if we trust in Jesus we'll join your Mama there

Now I've grown to manhood and I'm working this same farm
But every day I remember Daddy taking me by the arm
So son I know that we can't see to the far side of the hill
But yes I believe there's a heaven and Grand Pa's waiting still.

He's Gone

Losing a soul mate is difficult in any circumstance, but when you have been with that person for over fifty years, it is especially hard. I saw this unfold with my own mother, and it became another lesson in life that she taught me through example.

A year after my father passed away, she was still dealing with the loss. In conversation she would mention little details of her daily life and the things she missed most about my father. She had adopted small ways to help her through the day and reduce the loneliness.

After one of our conversations, I was worried that she was not letting go. The distance that separated us kept me from experiencing first hand the progress she was making. I placed the phone back in its cradle and wrote *He's Gone*.

She must have felt my unspoken concern because during our next call she told me that she was donating his cloths to the needy and removing some of his personal items that were constant reminders.

He's Gone

She sets his place at the table
When sitting to eat each meal
Pretends that he's still there
Doesn't know how to feel

It's been a year since he left her
But she can't believe he's gone
Still having one sided conversations
Like they did for oh so long

His pipe sits in the sun room
Where he loved to smoke
He's gone but she can't see it
Life's bitter silent joke

The Love His Children Share

Being close to a parent as they struggle through the latter years of their lives is tough. Sometimes we lose sight of the fact that the inconvenience to our busy schedules pales in comparison to the needs of our elderly parents.

Often, as I have seen first hand, the requests made of children are simply for companionship. A small task can become an immediate need because the parent just wants to see you, or needs to know that you are there. In cases such as this it's easy to feel put out, but if given a chance, moments like this can turn into sweet memories that are carried for the rest of our lives.

As my Father-in-law struggled with congestive heart failure and I saw him weaken with each passing day, things became clear to me in a way I didn't expect. As I drove to his house one afternoon *The Love His Children Share* filled my eyes. My visit became much more than a chore to be done.

The Love His Children Share

He calls his sons to chop wood
His daughter when he falls down
It's not so much he needs the help
He just wants them all around

It scares him that he might not wake
When he goes to sleep each night
But every time he hears their voice
Is another day that all is right

The bathroom seems so far away
When he struggles to get there
Afraid that he might fall again
It's a feeling he won't share

Never in his wildest dreams
Did he think that he'd be here
Calling his children for his needs
And hoping that they'll be there

Life once seemed so promising
He lived it full every day
Now he hangs on the telephone
And the words his doctors say

He thanks the Lord in nightly prayer
For the love his children share
As they smile and hold his hand
When they help him to his chair

Jesus hears this humble prayer
And knows that all is right
Because he's heard the heart break
Of his children's prayers tonight

This Last Mile

Ann and I moved to Nashville shortly after we were married, I was twenty four. This had always been Ann's home and all of her family was here. It made perfect sense to be with them. As the years went by, I drew closer and closer to her family, and especially to her parents. With the distance separating me from my own Mother and Father, they became much more than in-laws. They were my surrogate parents.

I was with them through their middle age years, retirement, and then old age. As this progression took place our roots intertwined and the relationship blossomed. We became family.

When they reached the latter part of their lives our supportive parents became feeble and frail. The ailments of age came upon them ever so slowly until finally the reality struck Ann and me that there had been a role reversal. Mr. and Mrs. Young needed us more than we now needed them. We had become the supporters and care givers.

The day finally came when it became unsafe for them to drive. It was a cruel day and their independence had taken a death blow. It was then that I realized that we were walking *This Last Mile* with two people that meant the world to us. My heart broke as I wrote for Ann what I knew she felt.

This Last Mile

I'll walk this mile with you
Hold your hand and see you through
Ever loving, I'll be there
Sooth your pain and give you care

You once carried me in your arms
Shielded me from all life's harms
Never wavered; you were there
All those memories we now share

Let's look back for this short while
Forget the pain and see the child
Life has brought us; you and me
From little one upon your knee

This last mile may be long
Lean on me; my arms are strong
Comforted in my embrace
Evening breeze; a feeble pace

When the shadows wither long
Close your eyes to my soft song
I'll shut mine too and see your smile,
Our final step in this last mile

Green Grass

My son lost his best friend to an IED in the AL Anbar province of Iraq. They had been best friends through middle school, high school, and beyond. On October 24th, 2006 at 10:00 A.M. Chris received a call from Richard's fiancé, Jen. Richard had been killed in action. His HumVee had been destroyed by an improvised explosive device. He had been in Iraq less than a month.

Chris now visits Richard's grave at the Veteran's Cemetery to talk with the friend he misses. Occasionally, Chris will be late returning from an errand or work and I will ask him where he has been. The solemn look on his face forecasts his answer as he replies "to see Richard."

The lack of grass on the grave bothers him, but I know that with the spring there will be renewed growth and a return of the green carpet over Richard's grave. One day, after Chris had visited Richard, I sensed the sadness in him. My heart ached, as my mind's eye saw him standing above the bare grave talking to his friend. As I prayed for healing, I somehow knew that just as time and the seasons would bring forth the *Green Grass*, so it would also bring healing to Chris. A poem was born in that thought.

Green Grass

Standing by the stone
Talking to a friend
Staring down at ground
Where green grass once had been

Family news given
Softly to a friend
Rests on hallowed ground
Where green grass once had been

Tears say I miss you
Falling to a friend
Soak into the ground
Where green grass once had been

Pure and White

On a snowy day in February Ann and I received the news that our very dear friends, Tommy and Becky Scott, had lost their 23 year old daughter Emmy in a tragic automobile accident. Emmy was taken from us while on a church trip in Arkansas. The car she was in skidded on ice directly into the path of a tractor trailer truck.

Ann and I wept when we heard the news, but we also prayed for God to comfort Tommy, Becky, Ben, and their family. Our faith in Jesus is where we go for solace, and it is also where Tommy and Becky find comfort as well. I have never known more godly people.

Emmy taught Sunday school at our church and served as a youth minister. She lived her life for God and taught numerous young people what it meant to be a Christian. She was a child and then woman of God.

I was sitting in my chair, quietly grieving and praying, when the words came to me. They came like snowflakes; one at a time. As they fell to me, I caught and then wrote them down. A poem emerged, *Pure and White*.

Pure and White

He laid a carpet pure and white
Across the hills and farms
The day he brought her home with him
And held her in his arms

She loved him dearly through the years
Gave all she had to give
Then served him faithfully with praise
Showed others how to live

From precious child to womanhood
She sang to him each day
Took his words into her heart
Forever there to stay

Now side by side they stand before
His father at the throne
As Jesus joyously proclaims
My sister has come home

Today we weep for children lost
To us for just a night
Praying we meet one blessed day
On a carpet pure and white

Sports

Spirit Wings

On days when things just seem to be spiraling out of control, I often take a mental retreat to a place I find comforting. This is a mini vacation from reality that helps me put the current events into perspective. On just such a day, I revisited the rice fields of Arkansas for a morning of duck hunting.

There is more to the experience than just shooting ducks, it is a reunion with nature, and the moments are precious. On this day I relived a foggy morning with two close friends, Johnny McAllister and Ron Jackson, as we shared the majesty of "Spirit Wings".

Spirit Wings

Enveloped in morning fog we sit
Speaking hushed in reverent tone
While ghostly shadows flutter overhead
Appear and then are gone

Spirit wings part misty sky
Gather wind then coast and sail
Hushed eyes strain in grey light dawn
Soft beating, swirling trail

Shrill whistle begs an answer now
From still bent rice below
Hanging loose in lanyards grasp
Hunter's call neglects to blow

A Young Man Stands In Football Spikes

When my son Chris was a freshman in high school, he played football on the freshman football team. This was not new; he had played many sports in the past. I had always been there on the sidelines or sitting in the bleachers cheering him on. However, this was a special year.

I guess I need to clarify one thing for the younger reader. Many men of my generation (baby boomers) refer to "cleats" as "spikes". We have done this since childhood and can use the terms interchangeably. Where today you would say "Ref, he cleated me!", in our younger days we would say "Ref, he spiked me!". Trust me, the pain was the same, and the Referee didn't care then either.

For fathers of grown children, who have watched their sons play sports from almost the moment they could walk, each of you has experienced the moment that I did when I wrote this poem.

A Young Man Stands in Football Spikes

Today son plays his football game.
I take my seat; it feels the same,
As seasons past when young boys clad
In bulky pads ran plays for Dad.

Now the freshman players appear.
The crowd stands up I hear the cheer.
I strain to see my little boy
Who's brought me so much pride and joy.

Onto the field runs a group of men
I'm shocked to stillness amid the din.
I see my son muscular and tall
"Franklin High School" the announcer's call.

He's grown to manhood over night.
I drink him in, a splendid sight.
Warm-up chants waft on the air,
How did I miss it, was I there?

Fathers see their sons as boys
Playing gleefully with their toys
Until one day reality strikes
And a young man stands in football spikes.

Thunder In The Ground

The running of the Iroquois Steeplechase occurs every May in Nashville. Ladies parade in sundresses and large hats, while the men dressed in sport coats, khaki pants, and the occasional straw hat lean against the fence rails to watch the horses leap over hedge or rail jumps.

The animals are magnificent athletes. They canter before the races, turning this way and that, adorned with colorful jockeys. Volunteers, astride their horses, trot through the infield dressed as if for a foxhunt, and hounds can be heard baying restlessly as they await their annual scamper down the home stretch. This is a wonderful day of tradition in Nashville.

While watching the winner of the Iroquois clear the final jumps and head down the home stretch, I saw in my mind's eye the famous horse Iroquois running stride for stride beside it, and the *Thunder in the Ground* made by heavy hooves gave birth to a poem.

Thunder in the Ground

Thunder rumbles in the ground
Press hard against the rail
Flaring nostril catches breath
Beyond the hedge they sail

Red and blue in stirrup leans
Head outstretched by the steed
Eyes roll white to catch a glimpse
Another of the breed

Fore hooves tear soft spring green
Coiled haunches follow through
Leaping into stride again
Crop bites it's now just two

Running neck with Iroquois
Lathering by the reins
Parting air above the rail
Against the bit he strains

Thunder rumbles in the ground
Spirit colors in the stretch
Fade back into history
Stand proud in artist's sketch

With You
(a poem for Rugby players)

On a crisp spring evening my son Chris was playing rugby. As an old rugby player myself, I watched with great interest and pride. In all truth, I was reliving a bit of my life through my son, although he is a much better player than I ever was. As I watched the game, two players came together head to head and a sickening sound of skulls colliding rang out across the field.

I watched from a distance as the two young men lay still on the ground and looked frantically for my son. Not finding him among the players gathering around their fallen comrades, I realized that one of the injured players was Chris.

I ran onto the field and sprinted towards him. Blood was everywhere and his coach had placed a towel over his face. I fearfully pulled the towel back to see two large lacerations surrounding his eye. He was hurt badly. Some people tend to panic in situations such as this, but I always seem to find myself inexplicably calm. I supervised as he was placed on a back board and loaded into an ambulance. We sped towards the trauma unit at Vanderbilt Hospital.

Hours later, my son's face stitched and facial fractures analyzed, we were allowed to go home. It was then that the terror of the event hit me and I was shaking. It took me days to regain my composure.

Several days later, I wrote *With You* as all of the pieces began to fall into place for me. The term "With You" is taken from the game of rugby, and is what players yell to a ball carrier when they are approaching him from behind. This lets him know without looking that they are there to take the pass from him.

With You

I split the gap but fullback's coming
Surely now I'll take a drumming.
Hard to cut in the morning dew
When close behind I hear "WITH YOU!"

Quick pass right without hesitation
Teammate takes the presentation.
Slipping past the fullback's grip
Safely on my downfield trip.

Years go by and son's on the pitch
I watch from the stands and feel the itch.
A vicious hit and I see blood spew
Held in my arms, "DAD'S WITH YOU".

To the hospital at a frantic pace
Stitches mend a broken face
Home to family, friends, and mates
Rugby now our life's shared fate

One distant day at a hospital bed
Son will await my final play with dread.
Remembering rugby times, just we two
And whisper in my ear "Dad I'm WITH YOU."

Chilkoot Pass

My youngest son Jim went to Alaska with his Boy Scout patrol and hiked the Chilkoot Pass. This is an ancient pass that was once the tribal land of the Chilkoot Indians, but later served as the primary pass into the Yukon Territory for the miners during the gold rush. Now the Chilkoot is a National Park on both the United States and Canadian sides. The trail through the pass has been maintained in its pristine condition. Only small groups of hikers are allowed onto the trail each day.

When son hiked the trail it was his first trip without me being there. Visions of grizzly bears and tumbles into mountain gorges haunted my dreams at night. In the end, he had a wonderful trip and old Dad was proud, but also a bit saddened that he was no longer a little boy.

I read everything I could get my hands on regarding the Chilkoot in an attempt at maintaining a connection with Jim while he was hiking. I wrote *Chilkoot Pass* to commemorate his passing from not only Alaska into Canada, but from childhood to manhood.

Chilkoot Pass

We walk in single file along
An ancient sacred trail
Where Indians and miners trod;
Their spirits still prevail.

Modern boots in rhythm with
The skin wrapped feet long past,
Thump like drums at distant fire;
Dancing images that last.

Discarded soles, like miner's dreams,
Lay scattered in the rocks
We hear their groans from heavy load;
Sweat dripping from their locks.

Flowers grow where warriors crept
Guarding sacred tribal land
Bow strings whisper in the wind;
Arrows slipping from the hand.

We see the vision of lost gold
Sparkling in the streams we cross
Shadowy panners, squatting low;
Hear the splash of slag they toss.

Today we hike to honor those
Who walked this trail before,
And leave no sign that we were here;
Dancing spirits and lost ore.

Coach Palmer

During our formative years there are always special people who make huge impacts on our lives. They may be teachers, scout leaders, pastors, or such. In the case of my oldest son Chris it was his high school football coach.

This man was exceptional. He was a godly person who saw the best in every boy and had a way of leading the young men he coached to discover the best in themselves. He was more than a football coach; he was a confidant, an advisor, a mentor. Like a father figure, he showed them what it took to be a good man. He was their father away from home.

When my son was going through those trying teenage years, this was an anchor. When my wife and I seemed to be too "parent like" my son would confide in Coach Palmer and he would steer him back to our point of view by explaining our behavior to him in terms that only a friend could use.

When Coach P. (as he is affectionately called) retired we mourned his loss as a family. It was more than losing a football coach; it was losing a member of our extended family. I only wish that every young man could have a Coach P. in his life.

Coach Palmer

When the whistle hangs silent by its cord
The last play written is gone from the board,
Coaches reflect on victories once won
Bitter losses "what more could I have done."

Real wins and losses are not on the field
in young men's lives true victory is sealed.
Players remember great coaches they say
For touching their lives in a special way.

The measure of a man is not in the sport
It's not in stats or newspaper report.
The odds are you won't know the role you played
When life-altering decisions were made.

But if you're lucky and God has a hand
One day in the street a player will stand.
He'll thank you for the difference you made,
Remembering you when he would have strayed.

Coach Palmer we know one such boy you touched
The life that you changed, one we love so much.
He will take your lessons till life is done
We thank you heart felt since he is our son.

Heavenly Rugby

I walked into the kitchen one evening and my wife handed me the newspaper, it was folded to the obituaries. She pointed out the picture and funeral announcement of a young man barely out of high school. As I read the announcement it became clear why she had brought this to my attention; he was a rugby player.

I volunteer time to high school rugby and enjoy the sport and the young guys who play it. I didn't recognize this young man, but his death took on new meaning, and the next morning I forwarded the article to his old high school coach.

Working along at my desk, an old familiar feeling started to rise in me and I couldn't shake it. By lunch time I knew that I had something to say and couldn't rest until I had given in to this need to write.

Rugby players are more fraternal than most athletes and this bond I felt for a young man I didn't know began to appear on my tablet. His obituary had recounted his love for the sport and that is all I needed to know. *Heavenly Rugby* flowed from my pen.

Heavenly Rugby

A rugby player died today
On distant pitch he is at play
Smiling as he makes each run
Rucking, tackling, having fun

I know when they finally beat my drum
He'll bind with me in heavenly scrum
And together we'll play the game we love
While angels cheer and fly above.

Until that day I'll remember his face
Each time I split the gap and race
Towards the posts to score a try
That he waits for me, my friend goodbye.

Family, Love, and Such

Pirates of White County

On a lazy summer day I was drifting back to life as a boy and the sheer joy of similar times. I remembered the fantasy and wonder that accompanied such afternoons.

There are places in Tennessee that bring the same feeling of wonder and adventure to mind that I experienced so many years ago. One such place is a deep gorge I visited while at my wife's family reunion in White County.

Suddenly I found myself there with young friends from long ago, and our pirate adventures were relived. We became the *Pirates of White County*.

Pirates of White County

In the shadows of White County
Where the mountain's roots intertwine
Ferns caress heads of moss
Beneath the ivy vines

Slipping between tawny toes
A stream bubbles and shines
Barely covering crawdad backs
Gurgles through leafy binds

Barefoot boys sit lazily
Poking sticks in rusty pails
Naming newts held prisoner
Beneath their pirate sails

Little Boys Inside

In email conversation with a good friend Paul VanDoren, he wrote that he had never really grown up. My reply to him was that there is a little boy inside each of us, and at that moment inspiration took control.

As a poem welled within me, I felt regret for all those times that I neglected the call of that little boy in me. Sometimes I get wrapped up in the apparent importance of my daily life and lose sight of the simple enjoyment that only a child can feel. Maybe it's my age and distance from childhood, but the need for such moments is much greater now… or perhaps I'm finally admitting my need to be that boy again.

Amazingly, being with a grandchild can make the rebirth of the *Little Boys Inside* us easier. Rolling on the floor with a giggling child has that effect.

Little Boys Inside

A little boy hid inside me
And begged for us to play
But there was always work to do
So I put him off another day

Now that days are getting few
Has he given up on me
Or is he playing hide and seek
Underneath the knowledge tree

I'll get a puppy just for him
Maybe then we both can play
Drop this tie by the riverside
Run in the last light of day

Little boys hide in each of us
They call "ALL-EE IN COME FREE!"
Fathers need to run with them
Heads back; laughing joyously

All Night Coals

As we grow older and the fire of youth subsides, our emotions change to accommodate this new level of maturity. You can look at this in many ways. Some chose to look at it like a river whose headwaters run swift and clear only to slow and deepen as they reach the sea. Personally I favor the analogy of fire. Fires are outwardly hot and bright when first kindled but change dramatically as dawn approaches.

Every couple who lives together long enough, goes through a transition in their relationship. When they are young and first married, couples are almost furious in their approach to life. Everything is happening <u>now</u> and is large in apparent importance. Whether it is finance, sex, religion, or any number of life events, life has a fever pace to it.

There is no single point of transition between youth and old age. The change is gradual and at different times in the relationship partners become aware of the happening. Sometimes they notice the difference simultaneously, but more often it happens that one partner realizes an evolution before the other does.

It was just such a catharsis that inspired the poem *All Night Coals*.

All Night Coals

Love don't last forever
Like it was when it was new
It's like our old stove
You've got to adjust the flu

You don't understand
Why things have changed so much
How huggin and squeezin
Have cooled to just a touch

If you look into my eyes
You'll see the difference too
That old fire has left behind
All night coals for you

All night coals burn deep
When the fire has gone cold
Like grandpa's love for grandma
Once they too grew old

Coals will see you through
The long cold nights of strife
So when the sun comes up
You can stoke the flame to life

Under all that ash
Is an old familiar glow
Waiting for your breath
And love to make it grow

Some say they burn out
When your life is through
But I know in my heart
They'll still be there for you

All night coals burn deep
When the fire has gone cold
Like grandpa's love for grandma
Once they too grew old

I Sleep Alone With You at Night

Some marriages stand the test of time while others fall prey to a distance that forms slowly as the years go by. A couple that Ann and I know separated and filed for divorce. After listening to the husband's story, it became clear that they had lost the intimacy in their relationship. Who knows how these things begin, but once they reach critical mass the outcome seems to be inevitable. Two people trapped in a relationship they can't, or won't, salvage.

I felt sorry for them. Anyone married for a length of time has had a fight over something or the other where they went to bed mad, but wished they could make up. Being a man I wrote the poem *I Sleep Alone with You at Night* from a husband's perspective, yet I am certain that it could have very easily been written from the wife's view point as well.

I Sleep Alone With You at Night

Where did the love go in our bed
How did we lose the lovers flame
Who do you see when you turn your head
Two lonely people, it's a shame

Listening while you comb your hair
Your sweet voice hums soft and low
When the lights out you're not there
Slipping into bed so slow

I sleep alone with you at night
Missing your body next to mine
Dreaming of days I held you tight
Making love at morning light

Where did the love go in our bed
Is it me you're longing for
Did you hear a word I said
Or just the closing of the door

You jerk at my gentle touch
Not tonight I'm just too tired
Your headache hurts way too much
Where's the love I once desired

I sleep alone with you at night
Missing your body next to mine
Dreaming of days I held you tight
Making love at morning light

This old bed may be too wide
And you too far away
But I'll dream you by my side
And right here I will stay

I sleep alone with you at night
Missing your body next to mine
Dreaming of days I held you tight
Making love at morning light

He Thought She Loved Him

I'm often amused and chuckle to myself when I see wealthy, high profile couples on television. There stands this mediocre or even down right ugly person with an incredibly good looking spouse. It isn't hard to figure out who has the money. Unlike in fairy tales, this was an ugly duckling that wasn't a swan at the end of the story; or a frog that never turned into a prince.

One morning I was sitting in the waiting room at my doctor's office, and noticed a magazine featuring the in depth story of a celebrity's failed marriage. I began to wonder if both of them actually saw the arranged nuptials in the same light, or if in fact one of them actually was in love.

The tragedy of such a one sided relationship isn't limited to the rich and famous. I began to ponder what it would feel like to be the "last one to know" in a lopsided marriage.

He Thought She Loved Him

He thought she loved him
The boy and his poem
But as it turned out
It was where he was going

She rode him all day
She rode him all night
She pulled on the rein
Made the golden bit bite

The boy wrote his verse
And winced at the spur
"Leave her", friends warned him
Yet he loved all the more

Lived in his castle
Never thought it fine
A servant he was
Slept alone over time

His ladder was climbed
He'd topped his last hill
She put him up wet
New steed; climbing still

She stroked her fair mount
He watched from the barn
As poetry sad
Coursed cold down stiff arm

He thought she loved him
Old man on his own
But as it turned out
She rode off alone

Small Things

Our hope is that with age comes wisdom. I found evidence of this in my sister Betty's new approach to life. After being such an intensely driven person since childhood, she found a new (at least to someone with a class A personality) way of maintaining her sanity.

She told me that she had become overwhelmed with life's many problems and that for her own peace of mind she had started looking for glory in the small things each day. A few examples followed, and I smiled at the simplicity of the plan. I even went so far as to try this myself… It worked! I found that I was happier and more at ease.

As a way of thanking Betty for this newly acquired perspective, I wrote *Small Things*. It is a small verse about small things that can make you enormously happy. Thanks for opening my eyes Sis.

Small Things

Find glory in the small things
When life overpowers you
Look for the first flower of spring
Or the glimmer of morning dew

Hear the soft purr from your kitten
As you scratch beneath his chin.
Feel the warmth of new mittens
Or cheer a saddened friend.

See the glow in a young child's face
When they learn something new.
Watch children finish a race
Or a baby smile at you

Search for bits of glory
And I think that you will find
A happy ending for every story
And that clouds are silver lined.

Her Quiet House

I make an effort to call my mother often. She lives by herself in a big house that once housed a large family. Now she lives alone with the memories of children running about and a bear-like husband smoking his pipe quietly on the deck.

She suffers from the ailments of age and doesn't get around like she used to, but whenever I call she greets me with such excitement that it makes me warm all over. She's my mother, my Mom, my Mama, and as we talk she plays many roles. On some subjects she talks to me like the grown man that I am, but on others I can here the tone of Mama talking to her little boy. I never complain; I love reliving those days too.

One afternoon I called her and she answered in a tired voice. I said "Hey Mom!" and she was instantly transformed. She was so excited to hear my voice, and it made me remember her reaction when we would come home from school. After our conversation I couldn't get the feeling of having rejuvenated her out of my mind. I could see her sitting alone in her house and the words began to form a picture of miraculous transformation and joy. *Her Quiet House* was born.

Her Quiet House

Granny sits in her quiet house, the same as yesterday,
Thinking of the times long past when the children played.
Now they're living adult lives with families of their own
But in her mind they're still babies and never really grown.

She misses that old man who passed away last year
No one there to call her name, she sheds another tear.
What a life they had together, now it's slipped away
All that's left are his memories; she'll see him this Sunday.

Sun shining in the window and leaves laying in the yard;
The simple things it seems have now become so hard.
Stooped in her back, shuffling stride; she rakes just to forget
The loneliness of nightfall; there's comfort in her sweat.

Here comes the afternoon school bus, same time every day
And she leans against the mailbox to watch the children play.
The falling leaves transform them into her precious own;
Running and skipping to greet her, glad that they are home.

Begging, "Mama I'm so hungry can I have a little snack?
Call me when it's ready I'm going to play out back."
But there are no children, no gleaming happy eyes.
She turns her back to the street so no one sees her cry.

A horn sounds from the corner. "Hey Granny" comes the call.
She beams and greets them warmly, "I was just thinking of ya'll".
Then just like clockwork, "Give Granny a big hug." She'll say,
As the silence is banished, for awhile, from her quiet house today.

The Whippoorwill

I'm certain that there was some thought that sparked the feelings that led to the birth of *The Whippoorwill*, but for the life of me I can't recall what it was. I was sitting alone one day and my mind was wandering (as it often does) when suddenly the inspiration came.

Somewhere in my subconscious a thought process was playing itself out, and eventually worked itself to the surface. When this happens I am always amazed, and often surprised at the direction it takes. Poems written at the bequest of such inspiration almost seem to have a life of their own and make you feel like you are reading someone else's work.

The Whippoorwill

The whippoorwill calls from over the hill
Past her house down in the hollow
Where love was found on a summer night
He's begging me to follow

But her daddy watches that old dirt road
This boy won't come a creeping
To meet his girl in the middle of the night
While everyone is sleeping

Don't call to me now ole whippoorwill
You know that I can't come
Her Daddy lays waiting on me
With anger and his gun

Tell my lover that she's all I see
Every time I close my eyes
And that sleep won't come to me tonight
As long as I hear your cries

When the sun comes up from over that hill
I'll slip down past the creek
And meet her fetching the morning water
To kiss her satin cheek

We'll make our plan to run off then
And meet up with the pastor
He'll marry us while the whippoorwill calls
And the moon shines alabaster

I'll build our cabin down in the hollow
Where we first dared to kiss
And the whippoorwill calls us home each night
To lay in lover's bliss

Twenty-four Years in the Making

Ann and I had been married twenty four years, and it was our anniversary. After so many years of giving gifts, I had run out of fresh ideas. Finally I settled on a practical gift. Ann had been looking at some very expensive kitchen accessories so this would be my offering. Despite her hint dropping, I was hesitant because this didn't seem very romantic and I had fallen prey to poor gift selection in the past.

As I drove back from the cooking store, I started thinking back over those twenty four years. I guess it was a combination of cooking accessories and love, but *Twenty Four years in the Making* began to materialize.

I had selected spatulas, a large wooden bowl, some wire whisks, and a set of salt and pepper mills. Don't ask me how, but they all showed up in the poem as I turned a mundane gift into a romantic one. All good cooks know that you can do wonders with presentation.

Twenty-Four Years in the Making

You stirred my heart on the night we met
Twenty-four years it hasn't stopped yet.
You were beautiful and sweet in the fire's glow
I had no idea how our love would grow.

You bowled me over when you said yes
I didn't deserve your heart I confess.
The sweet love you've given to me each day
Every man asks for when he kneels to pray.

I whipped you away from family and home
But you were not meant to travel or roam.
We moved back to Nashville one happy day
To make our new home, and never to stray.

The salt of your tears I've wiped away
Consoling and promising a better day.
As the sun rises and shines once more
I thank the lord for the girl I adore.

Like pepper and thyme you make life complete
Not bitter, not dull, not sour, and not sweet.
The perfect mix of all that is life
I love you dearly my wonderful wife.

A Glimpse of Heaven

I paced the hospital waiting room as my daughter suffered hours of labor. For nine months I had been wondering what my reaction and feelings would be the first time I met my granddaughter; my first grandchild.

Up until, and including this moment, I had been worried about my daughter and the health of the baby. I hadn't dealt with the fact that I would soon be a grandfather. The thought seemed so foreign. Was I really old enough for this to be happening? Would I feel the same love for a grandchild that I had felt for my own children? How would I feel when I held her for the first time?

I heard the intercom at the nurse's station excitedly proclaim that there was a baby coming. My heart started to race. This was it. Was my daughter OK? Was the baby OK? I could feel the sweat popping out on my forehead.

It seemed like life had just moved into slow motion. I watched the hallway and the clock on the wall. Each tick of the second hand took minutes. The nurses moved in and out of my daughter's room. I searched their faces for signs of what might be happening inside.

Finally the receptionist called my name and said that I could go back. I walked down the hallway to meet Jane Ann Girdler, the newest member of the family. I could feel my heart pounding as I opened the door.

There they were my daughter and granddaughter. The scene was angelic. I walked to the bedside and my daughter held Jane Ann up for me to hold.

A Glimpse of Heaven

I caught a glimpse of heaven
In her newborn eyes
Held her gently to me
Tiny little sighs

Skin as smooth as satin
Soft against my cheek
Little blue eyes open
Just to take a peek

Sudden jerk like falling
Granddad holds her tight
"Shhhh, my little angel,
You're safe with me tonight"

If time were to stop
At a moment such as this
I'd swear I was in heaven
Sweet smell, a cheek to kiss

Grandma's Song

I pulled into the driveway one summer evening and my headlights revealed my wife rocking our baby granddaughter in the hammock. As I walked up to them I could hear Ann singing and humming and it reminded me of days gone by when she would sing to our children.

It was a beautiful moment that still pops into my mind from time to time. Ann was looking down at our granddaughter and she in turn had her eyes fixed on Ann's face as she sang. I stood with them as our little one's eyes slowly closed. It was a wonderful evening.

Later, as the memory of that moment was playing through my mind, I found the words to *Grandma's Song*. Sometimes even the most carefully selected words are simply inadequate.

Grandma's Song

I sang an angel to sleep tonight
Rocked in my arms she's a beautiful sight
Eyes so blue and hair of brown
Love is what makes the world go round

Soft and low I sang sweet love's song
Forgotten lyrics as I hummed along
She didn't mind she just looked at me
And loved me right back in harmony

It doesn't matter what song I might sing
Her eyes are fixed on me as we swing
Grandma loves her little girl you see
She's my sweet baby, rocking under the tree

Oh so slowly she falls fast asleep
I hum another verse as the tree frogs peep
How could I feel more contented than this?
Precious baby to hold, mid summer night's bliss

Y'all Be Smart Now

Years ago in Mt. Airy, North Carolina, my brother Chuck and I would run barefooted over our grandfather's farm. There were no high tech toys back then; we would play with tobacco stick guns and make forts out of tobacco sleds. Life was simple and good.

Night was a special time. The family would gather from the fields to eat and rest. Following dinner the men and children would retreat to the yard where the men would lean back against the house on cane-bottom chairs and talk while the children played games.

Finally it would be time for bed, and as a child I slept on the floor on a palate made of quilts and covered by a sheet of soft cotton flour sacks (split and sewn together). As with children today, we wouldn't fall right to sleep. My brother and I would kick and laugh until we heard our grandpa yell *"Y'all be smart now."*

Y'all Be Smart Now

Summer night in sixty three
Palate on the floor for brother and me
We kick our feet
Underneath a flour sack sheet

Grandpa calls "Y'all be smart now"
Trying hard but we don't know how
We're rough neck boys
Trying not to make a noise

Window's open to catch a breeze
Leaves are still in the old oak trees
The night is hot
Thank you lord for all we've got

Summer nights still call to me
Close my eyes; little boys I see
Smiles on the floor
Back in Carolina once more

"Settle down, Y'all be smart now"
He'd be proud that I know how
I'm still tonight
Quiet thoughts before first light

Laying here in my fancy bed
Memories dancing in my head
I'd trade it all
Just to hear my Grandpa call

Uncle Wade

I had a special uncle on my mother's side that I always looked up to and admired. He was the son who stayed behind and ran the family farm. I don't know if his approach to life was because of his association with the farm, or if he chose the farm because of his approach to life, but he was a kind mind and carried a disproportionate burden when it came to family matters.

When I think of family duty, physical strength, character, and personal sacrifice, I always count my Uncle Wade Holyfield in the short list of people I think of. There are very few people that I classify as heroes, but my Uncle Wade is one of them. He died at the young age of fifty seven and I have missed him terribly.

In a moment of nostalgia, I was thinking about the wonderful childhood experiences on my Grandfather's farm. It is impossible for me to remember those times without remembering Wade. He was so intertwined with the farm that they can't be separated, even in thought. The memories began to form words and *Uncle Wade* became verse.

Uncle Wade

Overalls and a sweat stained hat
Sun worn face not an ounce of fat
Shirt smelled like a tobacco barn
Harness was hanging from his arm

Down to the creek I rode the mule
Bent to drink and I got schooled
Slid right into that water hole
Laugh every time the story is told

Smiled with his eyes when he saw me
Horsy rides upon his knee
Scolding when I'd wander off
Then hug me close and whisper soft

I looked up to my uncle Wade
A finer man was never made
Plow all day in the summer heat
Then lift me high right off my feet

Run to him coming home at night
He'd pat my back and squeeze me tight
I'd hug him hard around his neck
Beard was grizzly, but what the heck

With His Boots On

During a family dinner, my daughter Mariah was teasing her husband Mike about his mother's revelation that he slept with his new cowboy boots on when he was a boy. I could tell that he was a bit embarrassed until I confessed that I had slept with a new football helmet on when I was a boy.

That thought had escaped me for years. The joy of an important possession and the dreams of children are magical times for child and parent. The image stayed with me for several days as I enjoyed the memory.

While sitting in traffic, Mike's cowboy boots came back to me, and brought with them a vision of childhood and cowboys. Suddenly the words to *With His Boots On* poured over me, and I rode across the range… a little boy that had grown up.

With His Boots On

Pop's out on the front porch
In his old rocking chair
Eyes fixed on the sunset
Breaths deep the cooling air

Son rides with the cattle
Soon they'll be bedding down
He'll sleep with his boots on
A saddle on the ground

Mom looks out the window
Her hands still in the sink
Pink sunsets take her back
They always make her think

Son would put his horse up
And clamber into bed
He'd sleep with his boots on
After his prayers were said

That little cowpoke's kiss
Still lingers on her cheek
Tonight he shares this sky
Somewhere on Crooked Creek

A Cowboy lifts his eyes
The stars say day is gone
Thanks the Lord for this life
Then sleeps with his boots on

Let Him See Through Your Eyes

My father-in-law, Pop, was deathly ill. He had lost his ability to care for himself and his mind was confused. As I watched him go through this heartbreaking stage in his life, it made me think of my father who had passed away two years previous.

Due to distance and family obligations, I had not been able to visit my father as much as I should have. I thought about the time I had lost with him and the words that were never spoken. I often wondered if he understood my absence. I lived close by my mother and father-in-law. We saw each other frequently and they always knew what my family and I were dealing with. This was something that was lost with my parents.

I stood by Pop's bed and in a lucid moment he tearfully told me that he loved me and thought of me like a son. My eyes welled with the breaking of my heart. Later that evening I was staring at the ceiling wishing that sleep would come when then words to *Let Him See Through Your Eyes* came to me. Would Pop one day be able to tell my father of his son and the life that he had built so far from home?

Let Him See Through Your Eyes

When you meet my father
Give him news of his son
Let him see through your eyes
Just what I've become

When you sit together
And he asks about me
Tell him of grandchildren
Bounced high upon my knee

When you dine with angels
Whisper soft in his ear
The story of a husband
That loves his wife so dear

When you stand together
Bathed in holy majesty
Recount my love of God
One day his face I'll see

When you meet my father
Tell him of the son I am
Let him see through your eyes
The essence of this man

To my Father

Major Charles H. Forbes
August 9, 1921 – October 23, 2004

The Night My Hero Died

My father was a military man. During his career in the Army he served in both World War II, and Korea. His service to our country defined him and shaped his approach to life. However, the reality of his life's sacrifices, although never spoken, could be seen in his eyes during those private moments when he thought no one was looking.

As his son, he was my mentor, my role model, my hero. The quiet strength with which he approached life was an inspiration and his influence will forever live on in me. He was the child of past fathers, as I am, and my children are. This is the continuum of fatherhood.

Thanks Dad.

The Night My Hero Died

One fall night my hero died
Tried my best, but still I cried
Never felt so all alone
Moon above, but no light shone

Sat in the dark by myself
Listened, as the clock struck twelve
Looked down where my dog stood
Gave him a rub, like my hero would

He loved animals; who would have guessed
Of a warrior who had put so many to rest
Did those scenes of long ago battles
Haunt him at night when the windows rattle

A quiet man who didn't say much
Always hugged children; taught his sons such
A certain demeanor is expected towards men
But he was quick with a smile or a grin

A man is only as good as his word
A lesson I have often heard
From my hero, from father to son
If honor is challenged, you never run

When heroes fall the earth stands still
Shudders a bit as if with a chill
Because there's a void in the fabric of life
Worn by his friends, his children, his wife

We will do our best to darn the hole
Left by the man; with such a big soul
But the patch I know will always show through
Because you can never mend a father's loss in you.

Printed in the United States
107804LV00001B/343-372/P